THE KING'S PROTOCOL

THE KING'S PROTOCOL
HEARING *from* *the* KING

SEAN A. QUENTAL

TATE PUBLISHING
AND ENTERPRISES, LLC

Published by Tate Publishing & Enterprises, LLC
127 E. Trade Center Terrace | Mustang, Oklahoma 73064 USA
1.888.361.9473 | www.tatepublishing.com

Tate Publishing is committed to excellence in the publishing industry. The company reflects the philosophy established by the founders, based on Psalm 68:11,
"The Lord gave the word and great was the company of those who published it."

Book design copyright © 2014 by Tate Publishing, LLC. All rights reserved.
Interior design by Jake Muelle

Published in the United States of America

ISBN: 978-1-63063-172-7
1. Self-Help / Personal Growth / Happiness
2. Religion / Christian Life / Personal Growth
14.04.28

Contents

Introduction

Have you ever been afraid?
Welcome to the human race.

When you are afraid, it is almost impossible to concentrate on anything else. The same thing happens with sickness. When you're suffering, it's as if you have to concentrate on that. When you are worried about your own survival, solving the problem of survival comes first. Nothing else seems to matter in comparison.

While everybody knows this, we are not very good at helping one another with this reality. Have you ever had a well-meaning friend try to deal with your fear? Perhaps you were given such comforting words as: "Well, don't be afraid. I expect it'll all work out." Or my all time least favorite: "Get over it."

Was that helpful? Hardly! Did your friend walk away as if he or she had completely forgotten you? The person showed "sympathy" by agreeing that fear feels bad and then "solved" the problem by telling you not to feel it! Do you really accept that this kind of "comfort" is all a friend can offer?

Their advice is actually poor since they are saying that you should simply not feel what you are feeling.

Or did you have a friend who was wiser than that? This person did not tell you what to feel but instead paid special attention to what you actually felt. He or she presented evidence, offered support, and told you stories. This person worked with you until your fear subsided. Perhaps you had a friend who knew that telling you what to feel would not manufacture the "correct" feelings.

When you are afraid, which type of person do you prefer to be with?

Everyone I have ever asked that question to has chosen the second one, yet hardly anyone ever acts like that. You want to have a friend who is willing to spend time with you, addressing your feelings and helping to heal the hole inside your soul.

This type of friend does not tell you how or what to feel but instead pays special attention to what you are feeling and works upward from that foundation. I want to be that friend, the one that goes the extra mile and helps you back to physical, mental, and emotional clarity.

Several years ago, I was extremely ill. I consulted doctors and counselors and tried every cure in the book, including fasting for seventy-four days. But I wasn't healed until I made the amazing discovery that I'm going to share here. Mind you, I was no novice to healing or health; I'd started studying nutrition when I was twelve years old, some thirty-eight years ago.

If nutrition were the answer, I would have used it to solve my problem. I had access to pharmaceutical grade nutrition and owned a nutrition distribution company, long before the masses were taking supplements.

I also took practically every psychology class offered. That wasn't the answer. I got straight A's in anatomy and physiology in college, and I understand the body.

I have a doctorate from a seminary, so I know the biblical teachings on healing. I have studied every scripture on healing. You can't go to a school and learn what I am about to teach you; we have seen every type of disease healed, marriages restored, addictions completely disappear, and miracles, such as a leg growing three inches (www.thekingsprotocol.com). We have worked with every type of person: young, old, rich, poor, educated, and not educated.

Nationally, an average of five percent of people who attend a healing service receive a healing. Every person we have worked with has experienced a breakthrough—everyone! Sometimes it manifests as a healing, sometimes as a marriage restoration, other times as a miracle. The point is that the King is ready, willing, and able to listen to the requests of his people. There are other kingdom protocols to follow, but more on that later. Think of me in terms of the person that will escort you to meet the King. That escort will advise you of what you need to do to when you engage the King.

The King is the one who brings healing, and he has revealed to me his protocols for so many different areas in life. This book is the first in a series that will lay the groundwork of the King's protocol. It just simply works!

These discoveries transformed me. I became a completely new person, one who my old friends barely recognized, who was being changed into the likeness of Christ's image.

I know I am not the only person to have suffered—nor am I the only one to have been dramatically released from this kind of illness. My mess became my message, and you're going to see that here. I want to help you understand what I went through so that you can be released too. I want to help you walk this out, as I walked this out.

This book is not an instruction manual for what you ought to feel. It does not tell you "what to feel," although it displays the consequences of making wise choices—choices that might never have occurred to you before. This book presents evidence from neuropsychology, anatomy, physiology, the Word of God, and stories about real people just like you. This book was written to walk beside you if you are struggling with fear, stress, or other challenges—to be your friend.

Why, you ask? Because I can relate. I was tired of people telling me theory and telling me to have more faith, go to this conference or that conference, or go to this speaker when what they really meant was that they didn't have the answers. They were like the first group of people that tried to help by telling me not to feel a certain way.

I have taught this for over twenty years and people just kind of stared at me like deer in the headlights until recently, because there is a change taking place. I was about to give up teaching this and just do it privately until I attended a conference at a major church. All the speakers were trying to preach/teach on the mind-body-spirit connection.

Sadly, they didn't have the expertise to explain what I will explain to you in this book. I took them aside and enlightened them as to the process and the protocol—the King's protocol. One of them, a grandfather in the healing field, said to me "I want everything you have ever written and all your videos." They knew there was something they were missing. A lot of people have told me, "This is the piece I was looking for; it all makes sense now."

I was at another conference and the main speaker asked me to share my story with the MDs and Ph.Ds that were in attendance. They all had the same reaction: "Finally! We have the missing piece. We can work with our patients to a point, but they seem to 'get stuck.'"

This process has been duplicated over and over all over the world. Countless people have been set free and put what seemed to be impossible roadblocks to overcome behind them. I have stacks of emails from people who have seen me speak, have applied this process, and are now free. It works the same in Ireland, India, Kuwait, Australia, and even New Jersey. They followed the King's protocol.

Frankly, our society and the church are not very good at helping one another when it comes to dealing with fear, stress, and health challenges. You'll read some parts that are a little scientific because they come from college-grade courses. You will see "my heart" in this book, nothing more or less than the truth.

You may face a few challenges to your old beliefs—but rest assured, it will all be for the better. This book presents real-life stories about real people just like you seeing extraordinary results. This book was written to "walk beside you," to be that friend that goes the extra mile. The one, up until now, that you may have never had … but the one you always deserved, desired, wanted or wished for.

This book would have never been written without the help of two of my friends, Bruce and William. I am forever grateful to Bruce for the countless selfless hours he spent helping me get to the next level. He is an amazing man and I love him so much.

My friend, William Yarbrough, inspired me and is one of the smartest, most generous, tenderhearted men I have ever met. I have been working on this book for many years, and it was his insights that convinced me to complete it. Bill, you are my friend and I love you and Dianne so much.

We now have in place the ability to help many more people through this interactive book, the website, other technologies, and most importantly people who have been equipped to apply the King's Protocol specifically for your situation…" (www. thekingsprotocol.com)

Let's get started …

Chapter 1

Hearing from the King

I began each seminar, conference, or speaking engagement at church with these words:

> Although I was trained as a pastor, I'm not a pastor; I was a businessman. I'm the guy they would call on to help them when they had a problem. It has been this way since I was about sixteen years old. I was always helping people with problems. In business at twenty years old, I was trained by one of the best in the world, Michael Gerber, author of the E-myth series.
>
> I experienced a real-life trauma and I am going to share with you what I have learned. The trauma was incredibly painful, the toughest thing a man can go through.
>
> What you will hear today will not be theory; it is practical and powerful. It is time-tested and certain. It works everywhere on the planet. I had so-called incurable illnesses, and they are now gone. How many of you here would like to hear the voice of God in the next five minutes?

This worked for ninety-five percent of the people every time, everywhere. They all wanted *(Do you want to hear God? do you clearly want to hear the voice of the King?)* to hear God speaking. In five minutes, they clearly heard the voice of the King and acted on it. I had their attention, and God had their hearts.

I understand the King's protocol on how to hear his voice. On this very day you will hear God's voice; are you really ready?

Before I share that with you, I want to lay out the process so that you can understand it.

Parables are time-tested, effective ways of conveying a truth. Jesus used parables. When Jesus was asked directly why he used parables, He quoted Isaiah 6, and concluded. His response with, "So I should heal them."

> [13] Therefore I speak to them in parables, because seeing they do not see, and hearing they do not hear, nor do they understand. [14] And in them the prophecy of Isaiah is fulfilled, which says:
> 'Hearing you will hear and shall not understand,
> And seeing you will see and not perceive;
> [15] For the hearts of this people have grown dull.
> *Their* ears are hard of hearing,
> And their eyes they have closed,
> Lest they should see with *their* eyes and hear with *their* ears,
> Lest they should understand with *their* hearts and turn,
> So that I should[a] heal them.'[b]

> Matthew 13:13-15

Numerous researchers have clearly shown that 80-95% of all disease is thought-based.

Let's think of healing in terms of a mindset change or a paradigm shift.

My wife and I spent time discussing this with our friends Dr. Caroline Leaf and her wonderful husband Mac. Dr. Leaf is one of the world's top experts on the brain.

Dr. Caroline Leaf writes: "87% to 95% of the illnesses that plague us today are a direct result of our thought life. What we think about affects us physically and emotionally. It's an epidemic of toxic emotions."

So a parable is designed to quickly, efficiently change the way one thinks. Our brains are designed to respond to stories.

The book of Matthew has the highest concentration of parables in the Bible. There are forty-eight parables, and the thirty-ninth parable is called the "Unmerciful Servant." Jesus tells this parable:

> [23] Therefore the Kingdom of heaven is like a certain King who wanted to settle accounts with his servants. [24] And when he had begun to settle accounts, one was brought to him who owed him ten thousand talents. [25] But as he was not able to pay, his master commanded that he be sold, with his wife and children and all that he had, and that payment be made. [26] The servant therefore fell down before him, saying, 'Master, have patience with me, and I will pay you all.' [27] Then the master of that servant was moved with compassion, released him, and forgave him the debt.
>
> Matthew 18:23-27

This is the parable of the "Unmerciful Servant," a story Jesus gave to Peter to help him understand the true concept of what forgiveness was.

Peter thought it was quite generous and revolutionary to forgive his brother seven times. However, Jesus corrected him and multiplied that number—up to seventy times seven. He emphasized that true forgiveness eventually had no number, and it was obviously a concept that Peter had trouble reconciling. No doubt, this prompted Jesus to tell a story of a master and a servant.

The indebted servant begged his master for forgiveness, to which the master replied generously and canceled the debt. However, that servant went on to treat his fellow servants, who were also in debt, harshly. He made sure that the indebted servant under him lost everything, as he was sent to prison.

> [28] "But when the man left the King, he went to a fellow servant who owed him a few thousand dollars.[1] He grabbed him by the throat and demanded instant payment. [29] "His fellow servant fell down before him and begged for a little more time. 'Be patient with me, and I will pay it,' he pleaded. [30] But his creditor wouldn't wait. He had the man arrested and put in prison until the debt could be paid in full.
>
> Matt 18:28-29 NLT

When the master heard of this, he declared him wicked and asked him why the servant couldn't show the same mercy he had been shown. The master then handed the servant over to the jailers, who tormented him until he could pay back the debt that he once again owed.

Background reading on the subject indicates that Peter may have specifically had someone in mind when questioning Jesus about the principle of forgiveness. Furthermore, he was taking a Jewish perspective of the situation, keeping in mind the Mosaic Law, which very often assigned a number or a traditional protocol to handling a situation.

Therefore, Jesus's multiplication principle, which could also be seen as a redefining of the golden rule, probably shocked Peter, as it was essentially saying there is no limit to forgiveness. He said, "No, I don't say seven times. I say seventy times seven!" Obviously, that number has to be a metaphor for *an infinite number of times.* Yes, though a parable, the situation was largely a realistic example of human nature. While we ourselves beg for mercy and want to be forgiven, we are just as quick to judge the actions of others and to be harsh with our "debtors."

When the master was able to see the pathos, the inner feelings of the servant, he felt "compassion." This did not mean that he forgot the debt. In essence, he was able to separate the servant from the sin itself. The only way he could *forgive* was to separate the man from the situation.

It's easy for us to think of debt in terms of money, but we have to remember that a talent was not a dollar. A talent was a measure of weight used to measure gold or silver. One talent was seventy-five pounds, or as much as a man could carry.

I took the time to figure out how much this servant owed in today's US dollars. It equals $20,000,000,000—that's twenty billon dollars!

If you could somehow spare two hundred thousand a year, it would take a hundred thousand years to pay back your debt.

The point is it's an enormous amount of money.

A Hardened Heart

I had a neighbor who was the nicest guy you could ever meet. Everyone in town loved him; we called him the Mayor. One day, I talked to him and he told me about one of our neighbors that had wronged him, and then he grabbed his chest as he told me the story. I asked, "Why did you grab your chest?"

He said, "I get this pain in my chest when I talk about that neighbor."

I said, "Then you need to forgive him."

"I can't," he said. "I will never, ever forgive him!"

"Let me ask you a question," I replied. "If that neighbor was mentally ill, and did the exact same thing, would you be able to show compassion to him?"

He thought about it and answered. "You know, just last week I met someone like that. I felt sorry for him."

"What if I told you that neighbor of ours is mentally ill? Or what if I told you that he has a virus that is affecting his brain and his body and has left him potentially terminally ill. Would that change the way you feel about him?"

He thought about it. "I guess if I knew that he was suffering from a virus I would forgive him."

"So you see him differently when you separate the man, the being, from the 'virus,' the sickness that has made him this way. He is suffering," I assured my neighbor.

Then I asked him to close his eyes for a second, picture that neighbor, and try to separate him from his illness. He did, and I could see a certain peacefulness come across his face.

I asked him how his heart felt, and he replied, "Warm." Yes, the pain had melted away. All it took was the realization that the foolish man, the one he was once so angry about, had no idea of what he was really saying.

This warmth in his heart is due to the release of a chemical called ANF (see appendix).

So in less than three minutes he went from "*I can't* ; I will never, ever forgive him," to compassion and a healed heart—and, more importantly, peace.

Understanding "Protocol"

What this man did was apply "The King's protocol" just as described in Matthew 18. Here, we also see the King's protocol clearly explained. By definition, protocol refers to the customs and regulations dealing with diplomatic formality, precedence, and etiquette.

In the story of Esther, the young lady had to prepare for twelve months in order to meet with the king. The king had a certain protocol. She obeyed the protocol and saved the nation of Israel by following the protocol. She became queen through this process. The former Queen Vashti would not obey the king's request and was banished from the Kingdom.

If you want to ask for the King's mercy, or today, the queen's or the president's, then you have to follow a protocol. The very honor of speaking to such a person demands that you follow a protocol, lest you be escorted away and lose your privilege.

Therefore, the King's protocol can help keep matters in perspective, especially in terms of forgiving others. If God is the master, who has forgiven us for our sins, then he has provided a "protocol" of what is required to stay in his favor. Otherwise, he retains the right to throw us in "jail," just as the master had the power to do to the indebted slave.

Protocol Violated

> "Then his lord, after that he had called him, said unto him, 'O thou wicked servant, I forgave thee all that debt, because thou desiredst me: **Shouldest not thou also have had compassion on thy fellow servant, even as I had pity on thee?**' And his lord was wroth, and delivered him to the tormentors..."
>
> Matthew 18:32-34

The protocol here was clearly that the master expected the servant to show compassion, as he was shown patience. He was expected to take pity and show compassion to ones lower than him, just as the master did. When he *violated that protocol,* the master felt compelled to take away what was given to him in kind. When he failed to show the same compassion, the master exposed him to the fury of "tormentors."

What I take away most from the "Unmerciful Servant" parable is Jesus's perspective on the matter of forgiveness. We see right away that He *never used a secondary protocol*, as in "Do what I say, not what I do" or "This only applies when..." He always uses the *highest protocol* for whatever he did, holding the high and mighty to the same standards as the lowly and the weak. He lived this message, as we clearly see from other passages and parables, from the *golden rule*. He shared about *doing unto others* to the manner in which he died—praying for forgiveness for the men who put him to death.

Now someone's first reaction to this might well be, "But that's different! My situation is completely different from that of Jesus, and from the parable of the 'Unmerciful Servant'." Indeed, oftentimes our first reaction to hearing the King's protocol is to invent a secondary protocol. So let's go ahead and do that. Let's say that things in your situation are completely different and that the parable is not applicable to you.

As we move on into Chapter 2, we're going to discover why inventing secondary protocols never works in the long term.

Chapter 2

The Sickness of Fear

You could also think of protocol in another context: the medical protocol. When a doctor understands the root cause of an illness, he can quickly identify the symptoms and label the disease. For example, there is a disease called *beriberi*. It is a nervous system ailment caused by a lack of thiamine (vitamin B1) in the diet. Symptoms of beriberi include severe lethargy and fatigue, together with complications affecting the cardiovascular, nervous, muscular, and gastrointestinal systems. A doctor who sees these symptoms knows he is dealing with beriberi—especially if it occurs in a culture of malnutrition, where thiamine-rich foods are absent from the diet.

In the same way, the symptoms of resentment and unforgiveness are as easy to identify as those of beriberi. I am convinced that harboring unforgiveness causes *many* biological and psychological illnesses. Who we are on the outside is a reflection of who we are on the inside. The world-renowned Mayo Clinic agrees with this (Mayo Clinic, "Forgiveness").

What Are the Benefits of Forgiving Someone?

Letting go of grudges and bitterness can make way for compassion, kindness, and peace. Forgiveness can lead to:

- ❑ Healthier relationships
- ❑ Greater spiritual and psychological well-being

❑ Less anxiety, stress, and hostility

❑ Lower blood pressure

❑ Fewer symptoms of depression

❑ Lower risk of alcohol and substance abuse

Fight or Flight?

How would you feel if you met a wild lion while hiking? It's safe to say that you would tense up and go into full panic mode! This is what you might call the "fight or flight" instinct. It's the adrenaline inside, the important messages your brain sends to the hormone (endocrine) glands all over your body. The adrenal glands not only pump adrenaline but also noradrenalin, cortisol, and other hormones, all for the purpose of helping you to fight or retreat from imminent danger.

In essence, the hormones would be preparing you to deal with the threat, in this case, a lion. You would require super-alertness and super-movement, so first of all, oxygen is increased. Your lungs go into overdrive, gulping in more air, and your breathing becomes faster. Your heart is also beating faster so that your blood will pump oxygen around your body at top speed. You need super-powered muscles, so more blood is directed to your arm muscles (so you can fight) and your leg muscles (so you can flee).

That leaves less blood for your hands, feet, and skin surface, which explains why you suddenly feel cold. If by some chance you are attacked and your skin is sliced open in the fight, you are less likely to bleed to death. Not only that, but just to make sure you have a good view of the fight to take place (or the retreat you need to find), your pupils will enlarge to let in more light.

You will also need to sense your whole environment as well as you can, so every hair stands on end, giving you those famous *goose bumps*. To prevent you from overheating, your body is also keeping your sweat glands open, controlling temperature.

Your body and mind also know that conserving energy is vital, and so they will actually shut down non-essential body functions during an emergency, which might include digestion, salivation, and even your bladder, which is contracted and relaxed, which explains why some people urinate or defecate in their pants when very frightened.

We can see strong evidence that the human body was made to survive, and this "panic" mode, which helps to extend life and fight against threats, is what is possibly going to save you from such a threat.

All that super-energy, however, has to come from somewhere. That's what the hormone called noradrenalin does: it mobilizes all the body's stored resources so that the super-energy is created. The cortisol increases blood-glucose concentrations and then keeps them stable; calls up the protein reserves; maintains the fuel supply; conserves the glucose, salt, and water; and suppresses the production of white blood cells. Your body is now nicely balanced, with a kind of "damage control" that allows it to achieve the "superman" state that it needs to deal with the lion.

When you are able to evade or conquer the threat, you know, like Samson did, your body stops this "superman mode," and eventually your functions return to normal. The adrenal cortex stops producing corticosteroids. Though your body is feeling slightly traumatized (which explains the sick feeling you usually get), it will repair itself.

Fighting or Fleeing "Lions" In Your Own Life

While you might not encounter a lion today, we still have very lion-sized problems affecting us at every turn. While the super "survival" mode we discussed is capable of saving your life on that fateful day when you meet a real lion in real life, the fact of the matter is that constantly living in "fight or flight mode" is devastating to one's health.

When the stress is continuous and unremitting, cortisol continues to be released into your bloodstream. While you're all hyped up and ready to fight, disaster is occurring internally. Your body is stabilizing your blood-glucose concentrations; calling up your protein reserves; maintaining your fuel supply; conserving your glucose, salt, and water; and suppressing the production of white blood cells, or leukocytes. See the link on the website labeled "Fight or Flight;" in one minute it explains this process. www.thekingsprotocol.com

This is a major problem, as white blood cells are the building blocks of your immune system. These "fighters" are on your side, protecting you from all sorts of bacteria and viruses that will inevitably come in contact with you in a normal year's time.

So here is some disturbing news. Every time you feel "hate," every time you bottle up resentment, you are telling your body to go into fight or flight mode. Your poor body is revving up, sounding the alarm, and frantically working to conserve and protect—ready to fight or flee from an invisible enemy.

It's easy to see why this survival mode is important when you're fighting lions, running away from bad guys, or standing up for your family against an attacker. However, what good is it to be all keyed up just to argue or just because you're having conflicts at work or among family members?

That's several weeks of the fight-or-flight superman state, and several weeks of the cortisol suppressing the production of leukocytes. After the first four days, you will suffer from a serious shortage of leukocytes. Guess what happens when you are short on white blood cells? You become susceptible to physical harm—just like we stated at the outset. The internal process affects the external body.

The Difference Between Short-Term Stress and Long-Term Stress

So does this mean you have to become a mellow yellow type of person and never stress over anything again? Maybe you should just let people walk all over you and give yourself up to whatever hostile people you meet? No, it's just not practical to think you're going to live a completely stress-free life. Natural elements of life are going to involve stress, whether it's facing sickness, death, or conflicts with various people who have different opinions.

However, not every situation involving conflict is pumping you full of noradrenalin and sabotaging your immune system! Short-term stress is *supposed* to happen from time to time.

It is only by learning to cope with stress that we mature and grow in knowledge and understanding.

You might think of "good stress" in terms of an athlete in training. This is an example of short-term stress, as he or she is building muscle and improving his respiration. However, the athlete also knows when to take a break, when to rest, and how to efficiently divide his time between working out, eating, sleeping, and even enjoying him/herself.

When you are undergoing long-term, negative stress, it's like you're working out 24-7. Your trainer is yelling at you to stop moving and to take a break before your heart gives out. However, you're not listening … you keep pumping iron, against all logic, almost to the point of obsession. Something's got to give soon, and it's going to be you, my friend.

Three Stages of Stress

Stage 1–Alarm:

"Whenever I think about him [the person he's refusing to forgive], I get so upset. I can feel it in my chest. I feel like hitting him sometimes. He makes my blood boil! He's the last person I ever want to see."

Can you see what's happening here? The man is practically stating that he's in flight or fight mode. He's confessing hatred, and at the same time he's revealing his weakness.

Stage 2–Resistance:

"I have nothing to say to her [the one I refuse to forgive]. I can never forget what she did to me. In fact, I feel dead inside. She is dead to me. The whole situation doesn't even bother me anymore."

How deceptive to think that one has "moved on" when in fact he or she may be in the *Resistance Stage*: a point of extreme cortisol production, so much so that the body has adapted to the excessive production and is treating it like a drug that it has become resistant to. You're not *over it*, your body's reserves are actually being sucked up in vast, greedy quantities, far faster than you can easily replace them. The cortisol is still striKing at your leukocytes, which are being destroyed faster than you can produce new ones.

The problem is that you don't even feel stressed anymore. Your body has adapted to the permanent state of excited self-defense and is pumping out hormones constantly so you can swing at your invisible enemy. The warning signs are early on: a person who was formerly resentful, but who now inexplicably feels calmer even though they have not changed, nor has the situation, may be simply be in the resistant stage … moving ever closer to permanent physical damage. It is literally the calm before the storm.

Stage 3–Exhaustion:

"I am so tired. I'm tired all the time. I get sick so easily. And it's all his fault, the one who sinned against me."

Not only has this person revealed their mental exhaustion, but it's clear to see that she has become physically exhausted as well. Her body has been exhausted of reserves of protein, glucose, salt, and water. She has existed in the flight or fight stage for so long that her body is worn out, the immune system is weakened, and the body is practically unprotected—just waiting for a virus to come and cause permanent or even fatal damage. The exhaustion stage can easily turn into illness, perhaps even terminal illness. This is where you are at your most vulnerable. Being "superman" took such a heavy toll on your body's reserves that you could "mysteriously" become sick and even die. The super-powers that sustained you through your problems cease the minute you no longer need them, and your ordinary resources are all used up. Just to make the illustration a bit more vivid, think about the character Superman. With all that cortisol activity, you are turning yourself into a Superman … and unforgiveness is indeed the Kryptonite that is going to kill you.

Spirit, Soul, and Body

"I can forgive, sure, but I will never forget." That's what I always said. I said it to the point that I stopped thinking about it. What they did to me was unforgivable and that was that. I tried to move on, but all I really did was bury the past. I never spoke of it. Sometimes, I would see them; I would see their faces and become filled with rage. Then I just let it go. I thought I was doing fine.

One of the main points in the New Testament and in the writings of Paul is that spirit, soul, and body are all closely connected, if not identical. The ancient Greeks also wrote of a three-cord understanding of human motivation, namely, the body, mind and spirit. King Solomon called "the wisest of all men" wrote of this also.

> 12 A person standing alone can be attacked and defeated, but two can stand back-to-back and conquer. Three are even better, *for a triple-braided cord is not easily broken.*"

(Emphasis mine)
Ecc 4:12 NLT

The mind was what made us alive and separated us from the dead; the psyche or spirit distinguished people from animals, as in rationality; and the body is what unites all of these together. The fact that the soul and spirit were closely bound together was significant—and Christians were urged to love God with soul, mind, and body.

Likewise, today we can see evidence that the soul and spirit are still connected and that they can still influence the exterior body. When someone says "You hurt my feelings!" this strongly indicates that words are affecting not only the rational mind, but the very heart of a person, the body, and thus damage on all three levels is occurring.

In this figure, we can clearly see the amygdala (two of them, one on each side), which is considered the primary organ governing emotions. It is important to understand that the amygdala not only produces emotion but stores emotion—as in, memories of strong emotions.

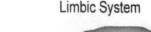

Limbic System

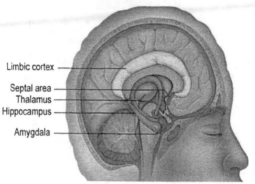

Limbic cortex
Septal area
Thalamus
Hippocampus
Amygdala

In fact, every emotion you experience and have ever experienced, is recorded as an "emotional record" in the amygdala. This organ helps you to learn and to avoid problematic situations, reinforcing negative emotions as meaning something dangerous. Meanwhile, the thalamus (also pictured) is the egg-shaped structure in the middle of your brain that works as a sort of routing station for all the messages that enter from all other parts of the brain. It puts the messages together and creates a "story," for which you will develop a non-conscious reaction and action.

The thalamus and amygdala work together to help you create reactions to new stimuli. The thalamus sends messages, creating a story (as in, this stimuli, while unfamiliar, reminds you of this other memory), and the amygdala then locates the emotional memory and helps you come up with an appropriate response. This process explains why smells, words, or images can sometimes conjure up feelings of sorrow, happiness, comfort, and mistrust. It can also cause problems if our emotional memory is tainted with episodes of distrust, trauma, violence, or other unforgivable incidents. In Chapter 3, we will delve into this further.

Chapter 3

Maturing in Thoughts and Feelings

C hildren do not act childishly only because of their lack of experience. A child's brain actually has a different structure of neurotransmitters. Neurotransmitters are chemicals that travel along pathways in your brain. The chemicals carry messages of information and have many more pathways than messages, so much so that there are many "dead end" pathways that do not match up to any other part of the brain and don't carry any particular message.

This internal "mess" actually slows down the neurotransmitters when they are carrying a message down a real pathway. And here is when adolescence truly starts: when a child's brain recognizes that it's full of a whole lot of pathways that it has never used and will never use again. The brain cuts back on millions of pathways that it doesn't need. The pathways left over suddenly become far more efficient. Now thought works faster, and abstract thinking, along with complexity, comes easier.

The Events of Childhood Shape Who You Become

It's important to remember that children are highly emotive and will associate emotion with most events. Therefore, just because a parent yells at a child to "Stop crying!" the child can't just accept the words; the emotion is all he/she is capable of processing.

Here's the thing: in trying to uncover the root of resentment and unforgiveness, we often discover that this harmful attitude does not result merely from cross words and localized conflicts—it is often indicative of past trauma.

When a child's mind processes danger, he/she will immediately and long-lastingly store emotions of fear, loss, and anger in the emotional memory section of the amygdala. Now, a seemingly minor event like a sight, a sound, or indeed, a conflict among friends can now trigger these negative emotions.

This is how trauma works. Perhaps you suffered a real trauma early in life, when your brain was immature. It might have been a truly horrible situation, such as the death of a parent or an attack by a dangerous animal. Then again, it could also have been something that was actually harmless, such as a sudden loud noise that your immature mind misinterpreted. Either way, this trauma is stored in your brain.

The thalamus can also cause problems in this regard, since it creates stories out of various data in order to help you produce a reaction. Even though the stimuli you experience may be peripherally related (i.e. a similar sound or color), the thalamus still has a job to do, and that is to detect similarities so you can develop an appropriate response. The thalamus can actually tell the amygdala that something is so close to a traumatic situation in the past that it's just as dangerous or negative. The bad emotions are triggered and stress is created.

While the traumatic experience might happen at any time in your life, it is much more common in early childhood. In your childhood, your undeveloped brain is also far more likely to misinterpret a situation and have an exaggerated reaction to fairly minor danger, loss, or frustration. Unfortunately, once you have this kind of emotional "mistake" stored in your brain, the mistaken response keeps on repeating.

Your brain has been locked into what we call "arrested development." Psychologists call it fixation. What happens next is truly a phenomenon of psychology: despite your actual age, your amygdala, working automatically, sends up the *same two-year-old's emotional response.* In essence, many of our motivations—the same ones other people describe as childish—*are childish.* They are remnants left over from childhood emotional memories.

Similarly, an immature thalamus can also make a bad "match" and report a false similarity, leading the amygdala to overreact. The tough question to ask is, "Could a trauma from your childhood be sending the wrong messages all over your brain and interfering with your life as a rational adult?" See website for video of how this works.

Windows of a Soul

Here is a real life story to explain how this works. A thirty year old mother of three came to our teaching, weeks later my wife and I met with her privately. She had many health problems. On the cusp of divorce, her home was in constant chaos. Each morning around two, she would go room to room and lock every window in her home; this is after locking them and checking them multiply times prior to going to bed. She had not slept for more than a couple of hours in a row for at least twenty years.

After spending time with her, helping her, right in front of us, she was shown the root of this irrational behavior. She described it as a hologram, a 3-D view of the scene.

At age eight, a neighbor had sexually molested her. After running to the safety of her home, she saw that neighbor looking into the home from a window. From that date to the day this was revealed to her, she had only a few childhood memories. All she could recall was about five memories as a child.

She applied the King's protocol right in front of us and was forever changed. No more late night irrational repetitive double and triple checking of the windows. The child had moved on from the childhood memory that was so traumatic that it was blocked out along with a decade of other memories. When we followed up with her, lasting peace had come to their home. She was a new person sleeping like a baby, loving her husband and children.

Can you imagine each time this woman looked at or out a window, her brain fired a signal to protect her from this monster? In minutes the king had healed her and set her free of childhood trauma and all its devastation. If we had applied the secondary protocol of "get over it," or hadn't been her friend, who knows how long this torment would have gone on. Medication was the doctor's protocol prior to meeting us. Free of all medication and peace in her home, she is now free to become who God intended her to be.

I have to mention one more thing that happened. While she was applying the King's protocol, her head had been down, she looked up at us. My wife and I simultaneously, out-loud, gasped as we saw her face change right in front of us. She was stunning! Beautiful. The former tormented, gnarled, tired, wrinkled servant was changed. The wrinkles were gone and she had de-aged about ten years. It was amazing; we will never forget that moment. That was not an isolated moment we have seen this "de-aging" process repeatedly. Proof positive, the King can indeed "renew your youth".

Alien Thoughts and Ideas

One thing that contributes to stress and to the attitude of unforgiveness is our thoughts. We always hear about toxic thoughts and freeing our minds of negative thoughts...but what are thoughts?

A thought is not a material object in a brain; rather, it's a movement. One neuron sends an electric signal to another neuron inside your brain. You repeat a thought by repeating the same electric signal, which triggers chemicals to move down the same communication pathway inside your brain. So naturally, you may wonder, "How do your neurons learn to make certain signals? Why do you think of some things more than others?" Thoughts are not random, contrary to what you may have heard. Thoughts actually do come from specific stimuli, namely, your own experiences. You cannot suddenly think about something that you've never learned about— unless of course you're receiving a heavenly epiphany! Or an un-heavenly communication.

Brainwaves or thought movements are electric signals of varying strengths and speeds. The experts group brainwaves into various types according to how strong they are and how fast they are moving. Weak, fast brainwaves, called beta waves, mean you are alert and active and able to think logically. Strong, slow brainwaves, called delta waves, mean you are sleeping deeply and taking a complete break from any kind of thinking.

Theta brainwaves, which are moderately strong and moderately slow, occur when you are deeply relaxed or in light sleep. When your brainwaves are at theta-strength, you don't have control over your thoughts; they enter your mind with you barely aware of them. Your defenses are down and you are certainly not considering them critically.

When your mind is in a theta state, you can have bursts of creativity, irrational pairings of unrelated ideas, vivid visual imagery, and a sudden capacity for rote learning. When your brain is in a theta-state, it isn't "in gear," and that is when the spirit realm can "speak" to you.

Now ask yourself, when are you at your most vulnerable? It's probably not in the beta stage, when you are alert and rational and can fathom the King's protocol with relative ease. No, you are most vulnerable when you are half asleep, perfectly relaxed, and when strange and "alien" imagery can infiltrate your mind. And, not so coincidentally, this is when wrong ideas and consuming hate can fester in your mind.

It is not exaggeration to say that alien or demonic forces may be preying upon your mind during these vulnerable stages and multiplying hate, even as Christ multiplied forgiveness, by sending you unhealthy, hateful thoughts about those whom you could not forgive. Do you remember in Job, when Eliphaz the Temanite actually confessed his mind's vulnerability? Read Job 4:13-16. You might be surprised at how accurately this passage describes the highly vulnerable theta stage.

He is describing theta brain wave activity

> [12] "Now a word was secretly brought to me,
> And my ear received a whisper of it.
> [13] In disquieting thoughts from the visions of the night,
> When deep sleep falls on men,
> [14] Fear came upon me, and trembling,
> Which made all my bones shake.
> [15] Then a spirit passed before my face;
> The hair on my body stood up.
> [16] It stood still,
> But I could not discern its appearance.
> A form *was* before my eyes;
> *There was* silence;
> Then I heard a voice *saying…*

Types of Memory

Visual Registry:

This visual memory only lasts about a half second, which is just about right, since you don't want to keep seeing things that aren't there!

Audio Registry:

This lasts about three seconds and helps you remember sounds, including words people are speaking to you.

Short Term Memory:

This lasts about thirty seconds and it is only used to accomplish an immediate task.

Long-Term Memory or Learning:

This is what you permanently retain, and it is difficult to learn something. Sometimes it takes years to remember something permanently, at which point you will likely remember it for the rest of your life.

By repeating thoughts and learning new thoughts by way of artful repetition, the thought keeps repeating its electro-chemical pathway through your brain, and that pathway becomes more and more deeply etched on your brain structure. Now that it has been engraved, it becomes easier and easier to recall that thought and set it running through your brain yet again. Finally, it is part of your neural structure and influences your non-conscious.

Identify the Trigger

The Power of Habits

There's one more brain part to meet: The hypothalamus. The hypothalamus is a tiny structure deep inside your brain and it controls automatic functions, such as heartbeat and breathing. It also interprets whether you're going to sense fear or not. If you're lying awake at night, rigid with unquiet thoughts, it's because the hypothalamus is sensing something and sending the *fear* message. Identifying the trigger and ceasing non-conscious reactions to events is one of the crucial steps to separating yourself, and your feelings about other people, from the fear and the resentment that is taking over your life. In review, consider the three parts of the brain we learned about:

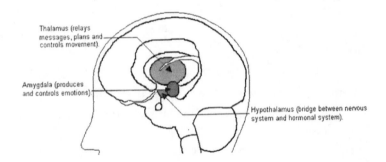

Now if it's this easy for a human like me to explain the way the brain works, isn't it logical to assume that alien or enemy forces can just as easily exploit this knowledge of the brain and manipulate you to experience these negative and life-threatening emotions?

As we move into Chapter 4, we are going to discuss the best way to cure yourself of these spiritual and deeply internal ailments—not just for the sake of the King's protocol, but indeed, to preserve your physical and eternal life. And also to gain your rewards in Heaven. If you are healed you will have more rewards.

Chapter 4

What Lies at the Heart of Bitterness?

Long ago, the Apostle Paul defined what lay at the root of bitterness. In Hebrews 12:15, he stated that if we do not hold closely to God's grace, a root of bitterness may spring up and trouble us. Bitter "roots" have the ability to bear negative fruits and defile us *and* other people.

Let's revisit how it happens. It starts simple enough, with something quite ordinary going extremely wrong. Maybe someone at work slams your project or a family member criticizes you. A hurtful memory is stimulated. It brings up all the angry feelings. You're tempted to retaliate. You might even "displace" your anger and retaliate to a third person that had nothing to do with the trigger. If you do this, the problem is spread around.

Of course, the person whom you've snubbed, being only human, also has a store of painful memories. So your angry words have also triggered *his* angry feelings. And if he's no better than you are, off he goes and takes out his aggression on a fourth person. So a chain reaction erupts. Many people are defiled.

The Hierarchy of Bitterness

Not only will unforgiveness affect your body, but it will also affect your mind. When you choose a path of unforgiveness, your body will decrease its production of serotonin. Serotonin is a neurotransmitter that produces feelings of calmness and wellbeing in your brain. If you don't have enough serotonin, you feel depressed or anxious.

Consider this diagram, which shows that there is an entire hierarchy to this general feeling of bitterness. Isn't this a thought-provoking scale?

It starts with *unforgiveness*, the first consequence, when someone says, "I'm not willing to forgive the offense against me." You start stewing on it, which reinforces the bitter memories. The bitterness becomes synthesized into your neural structure. Once that happens, any trigger can stimulate the memories into painful life. On the contrary, if you had no bitterness left, no amount of "triggering" could stimulate a bad reaction.

When you dwell on the flashbacks, you start keeping a record of wrongs. Tallying up exactly how much the other person owes you is the very definition of *resentment*—which is the second consequence. Have you ever heard anyone say, "On a Sunday afternoon back in April 1952, Aunt Barbara was sitting on the leather sofa wearing a pearl necklace and blue heels, and she told me off for biting my nails, and then she said…" That's resentment.

When you articulate just how much Aunt Barbara owes you, you start wanting to exact your due payment. You start telling yourself it's your right to get even. And so you plan your *retaliation*. That's the third consequence.

You don't plan retaliation without a fair amount of emotional investment. And what's the emotion? Love? Joy? Serenity? No, the emotion that propels revenge is an aggressive *anger*—the fourth consequence. Will you be expressing that anger? Yes, other people will know you are angry by the cross of your brows, the tone of your voice, and the clench of your fists. If you can *feel* the anger, then you can be sure that the cortisol is exploding around your body and that it has a physical manifestation.

Dwelling on the anger leads to *hatred*. This fifth consequence is a very, very dangerous one. You really couldn't care less about your enemy's welfare. In fact, you rather hope he will come to harm. This is where divorce comes in and I'm not just talking about spouses! Hatred says this: "You and I can't be at the same place at the same time. You need to leave or I need to leave." If we feel this way and speak the words out loud, the idea is processed and the proteins are synthesized. It becomes a self-fulfilling prophecy.

If you don't eliminate the hatred, it's a frighteningly short step to the sixth consequence. You don't just *hope* for harm, but you actually perpetrate the *violence* yourself. You slam doors, scream, throw cups, and eventually even punch people.

How much violence can you commit before you strike harder than you intended to? If you continue to the final consequence, you could finish with *murder*. Remember what Jesus said in Matthew 5:21-22, that the true sin was not just murder—as in Cain finally following through and killing Abel. No, the thought is where the sin started, as in "Whosoever is angry with his brother without a cause shall be in danger of the judgment." Even if you think you are not up to literally snuffing out a person's biological life, there is still verbal murder. If you assassinate a person's character with gossip, it is a form of verbal murder—assault. That's something that is beneath you as a happy and healthy individual in a good relationship with God.

The Tormentors

Now let's consider who the "tormentors" are in the King's protocol, or the "Unmerciful Servant" parable. Remember, in the passage, the forgiven servant goes out and finds his "friend." He grabs him by the throat. The words he says are simply, "Pay me what thou owest," but look at the context. Here we see him already past the basic stages of bitterness, almost to the point of murder.

So then the master was furious and delivered him to the tormentors or jailers, until he paid his debt in full. "Tormentor," a translation of the Greek word *basanistes*, is an Old English word meaning "one who elicits the truth by the use of the rack." When a medieval politician decided that an enemy spy or religious heretic was hiding information, the victim was tied to a *rack* and stretched. Limbs were dislocated from sockets, muscles were ripped apart, and skin was stripped off. Victims who survived the rack were often unable to walk or even to lift their hands. The word *basanistes* is used only once in the entire New Testament. Various translations render it as *tormentor*, *torturer*, or *jailer*. It presumably assumes that the jailer was assigned the task of torturing the hypocritical servant!

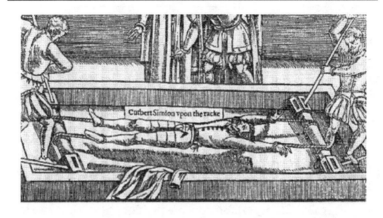

And yet, when we ride the scale of bitterness, the gradually evolving hierarchy, we are indeed left to the tormenters. Obviously, God does not hand us over to mere human rack-turners. However, it is a fitting metaphor for the internal torture that lies ahead.

Ephesians 4:26-27 says, "Be angry, and do not sin: do not let the sun go down on your wrath, nor give place to the devil." Yes, when we harbor bitterness, we are inviting the devil into our space and making it easy for him to take advantage of us—influencing our thoughts and multiplying "bitterness" torturing us with our own negative emotions.

Have you ever suffered from physical pain with no obvious organic cause? Have you ever suffered from mental or emotional anguish? Did you ever pray for relief from spiritual oppression, yet no relief came? Perhaps the evil force invaded your mind and body because you invited it right in! Perhaps it is taunting and sneering at you with the words, "I have every right to be here! The great King allows me to enter here, as he warned in Matthew 18:34-35."

"And his lord was wroth, and delivered him to the *tormentors*, till he should pay all that was due unto him. So likewise shall my heavenly Father *do also unto you*, if ye from your hearts forgive not every one his brother their trespasses."

I have a personal invitation from you because you are holding on to bitterness! And the only way to be liberated from this kind of torment is to forgive from your heart.

A woman came to us with the skin on her legs being ripped off. Years ago, when we were teaching at a larger church in New England, a woman who had attended the series of teachings set up an appointment with us. She told us how she was spending $1026 per month on medication. She told us a long list of aliments.

The most recent one was unexplainable to the doctors: the skin on her legs was peeling off as if it were being ripped off. Doctors call diseases with unknown causes "syndromes." This was indeed a syndrome. I "heard" from the King as she was talking to us. It was clear and concise: "She has unforgiveness towards her husband over a sexual issue." I presented that to her, and she said, "You are right, I'm really mad at him over that."

It took a few minutes for her to separate her husband from the sin and forgive from her heart, but she did and forgave him. She came back a few weeks later. The mysterious disease had left just as quickly as it had appeared. She told the doctors she had forgiven her husband and they said, "Oh yes, sometimes that happens."

The tormentors had no right to her anymore. She was so thrilled months later as she told us her doctor had taken her off all but one medication. She decided to donate the $1026 she was spending on medicine to a ministry. Touché—no more tormentors, and the money was hers to keep or do with as she pleased. I tell this story a lot because it isn't a coincidence that she followed the protocol and was released from the tormentors.

A Personal Story

Our family physician, let's call her Dr. Blinker, once misdiagnosed one of our daughters. The doctor said that there was nothing wrong and the apparent symptoms didn't mean anything. Then our daughter's appendix ruptured and burst, and she had to be rushed to hospital for emergency surgery. It was a very dangerous condition.

Given the denial of Dr. Blinker, I did wonder if my daughter's illness could really be something as commonplace as appendicitis. When I asked the specialist, he said, "There is no doubt. Any first-year med student could have diagnosed this. It is one of the simplest diagnoses there is—your doctor just missed it."

You can imagine that I was pretty annoyed with Dr. Blinker after I heard that! Our daughter was shunted to the operating theatre, and her parents waited outside. As soon as the surgeon emerged from the operating theater, I asked what on earth was going on.

The surgeon reported, "There was fecal matter everywhere in the intestines. It was a dangerous situation but we got it all." I asked him again about the misdiagnosis. He looked at me and said, "Son, I've been at this twenty years, and this was a simple misdiagnosis. Don't ask me again how such a mistake could have been made. Your daughter could have died, but she is safe now."

Clear-cut, wouldn't you think? My daughter had had appendicitis. That was the word of the experts who had opened her up to save her life. They had seen the ruptured appendix and they had seen the mess it made of their patient's intestines.

Yet when I went back to Dr. Blinker and told her about the misdiagnosis, *she defended her position.* It couldn't have been appendicitis, she claimed, because *she* hadn't seen it! Whatever a person claims, her words do not make it so. *Dr. Blinker was and still is wrong, and she nearly killed my daughter!*

Do you see the similarities? When we see symptoms of spiritual disorders, we often know from long experience exactly what the problem is. Yet people who are less experienced in this field cannot see it, and usually the affected person cannot see it either. It's like a virus on a computer. When they do recognize the cause of their disorder and act on it, they experience a lasting life change.

Remember, bitterness is injected into your mind by an alien invader. You meditate on the thought. You turn a short-term memory into a long-term memory. This long-term memory is a physical structure in your brain cells. It becomes part of your soul, thought processes, and part of your body.

Because everyone has been invaded by some of these alien thoughts, we can all trigger each other's bad memories. So we have an encounter with someone else, and this triggers a repeat of the memory. The more often you travel down this neural pathway, the thicker and deeper it grows.

Bitterness becomes so much a part of you that you assume it is you. It's just like the family physician's treacherous defense of her original misdiagnosis, when she defended bitterness as if it is somehow justified or healthy. Just as the physician assumed that she must be right, you become so convinced that your assumption must be true. You cannot see how your own bitterness might have caused your visible disorder; it has become a blind spot. It is crystal-clear to me that if you are suffering torment, you are harboring unforgiveness. This is what we're going to talk about in the final chapter.

Chapter 5

Experience Prosperity from the King's Protocol

There was a pastor to whom I taught the process of forgiving over a period of months. In the beginning, he resisted the whole concept. This is quite common for a person who has been trained without the understanding of the body, mind, and spirit. So far, none of their arguments against this concept have ever held up, and I have yet to meet one of these objectors who is successful in the healing field.

Eventually the pastor began to accept the body-mind-spirit connection and began applying the process of forgiveness. Here are that pastor's own words about how forgiveness changed his life.

> "Since I have implemented the daily habit of forgiving others and myself, I have experienced significant healing. I've been healed of chronic fatigue syndrome, allergies, insomnia, neck and back problems, grinding my teeth while sleeping, hypoglycemia, immune system deficiencies, acne, and skin problems.
>
> What's interesting is that I never even set out to get rid of these health issues. I wasn't aware that bitterness and/or forgiving actually affected my body! It felt so good to finally be released from the oppressive and destructive claws of these illnesses. Words can never describe how excited I am to wake up every day with a heart and body full of forgiveness."

Teach Me How to Forgive

There is only one issue left to discuss, and it is the most crucial lesson of all: how can you learn to forgive if everything in your mind, body, and soul is resisting the notion?

Forgiveness is difficult for two reasons: the natural reason and the unnatural reason. The natural reason is that we don't *want* to forgive. The unnatural reason is that we don't understand the nature of forgiveness. We sometimes make wrong assumptions about what forgiveness really means.

Remember that with evil things God cannot be tried, so don't confuse this to mean that forgiveness means *approving of the sin*. It does not. You don't forgive a bank robber by saying, "That's okay. There's nothing so very bad about stealing." Perhaps your fellow "servant" only owes you ten grand, but it is *not* all right to borrow ten grand without any intention of paying it back. In the parable, the slave did want to pay that money back, in all honesty. The whole point of forgiveness is that sin must be labeled as sinful.

Forgiveness is Separation

Remember what we discussed: sometimes the only way we can forgive a heinous and sinful act against us is to separate the sinner from the sin. You don't accept or approve the sin at all; you accept and approve the person and condemn the sin. Of course, your enemy doesn't *deserve* your acceptance, approval, or forgiveness. Remember, though, that strictly speaking, nobody ever *deserves* to be forgiven. Forgiveness is not about what we deserve.

In the parable of the "Unforgiving Servant," we see the King do three things.

1. Compassion

The Master, the King, is so moved by the distress of a man who is about to lose his family and be sold into slavery that he completely overlooks his twenty billion dollar debt. This King has a "people first" agenda, realizing that a human being matters more than anything that might be owed.

It's easy enough to say that when the *anything* is just money—and far more money than any of us are realistically going to see in our lifetimes. However, the financial debt represents *sin*. It indicates that the servant has done real harm to other people. Despite the suffering of anyone he might have harmed in the past, the King still cares about *his* suffering. Would you have compassion on a slave-trader, a drug lord, a torturer, or a mass murderer? These are the ones who have truly caused great loss. Yet, *whatever* those people have done, God places their status as human beings ahead of their evil deeds. It is the King's protocol, after all—the logic he uses to forgive us.

2. Separation

Secondly, the King separates the servant from his debt. The bills are taken out of his hands and tossed to the far side of the room. The King looks at his servant; He doesn't look at the debt. What does your Heavenly Father see when he looks at you? Paul tells us that this is your factory setting. In Ephesians 1, "Accordingly, He has chosen us in Him before the foundations of the world, that we should be holy and without blame before Him in love." God can see you this way because He looks at you separately from your sin!

I was once sitting in the audience listening to a Bible teacher when the Holy Spirit showed me something that I'm going to show you. I was struggling to forgive the most traumatic offense that a married person can suffer. I was in the middle of the heartbreak, and I was working through the issue of unforgiveness. Up until that moment, I had always seen the person that committed the offense toward me as one with sin. However, that day was when the Holy Spirit showed me this vision.

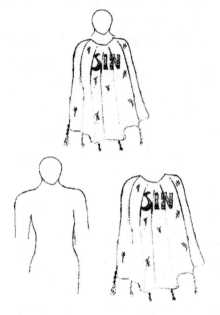

In the past, I saw the person wearing the sin like a cloak. The person and the sin were like one entity. Forgiving the person felt like condoning the sin.

I "heard" in my spirit the words: "You need to forgive the silhouette, not the sin."

That moment, my life changed forever.

3. Forgiveness

Thirdly, the King forgives the servant. The bills are destroyed, never to be paid. The servant is sent home, free to do what he likes. In my vision, I looked at the silhouette and not at the cloak, and I could say it. "I forgive you. I forgive you. I forgive you." And I was free.

Have you ever felt bitterness towards somebody and felt that knot in your stomach or a little ping going off in your stomach whenever you're around that person? When I see this person, that bitter ping has now gone. That's happened because I can separate the person from the bad actions. I'm free of the twenty-billion-dollar debt.

So what happens when the bitterness wells up again? Do you make excuses for it? No. We've already established that the bitterness isn't part of you, so there's no point in defending it as if it's you. Rather than let the bitter feelings trap you, it's better to get rid of them. If you slide back into unforgiveness, you can visualize separating the person from the sin-cloak—again and again, as many times as you need to. This is how you set yourself free from the prison, the torment, of unforgiveness.

Taking Bad Thoughts Captive

Have you ever asked yourself, "Where did that thought come from? Why am I suddenly thinking about *that* again?" Actually, we know exactly why these old thoughts return. It was simply because the thoughts were *there*, stored in your neural pathways. And they decided it was their turn to be noticed again.

When the neuron wants to send a message, an electric current runs down the axon. When the electric message reaches the fibers at the end of the axon, it stimulates those blue button-like shapes at the end, which are called *terminal buttons*. They then send out a chemical message to the next neuron. The dendrites of the next neuron pick up the chemicals, which triggers the next electric signal. And so the process continues. The message travels through thousands of neurons, until it reaches the end of the neural pathway.

These neurons need sugar, oxygen, and stimulation to live. When you eat, you supply the sugar. If you keep breathing, you supply the oxygen. The third thing you need to keep your neurons is *stimulation*. If you keep stimulating a thought by repeating it, it burns its neural pathway more deeply in your brain, and it stays. Thoughts that you don't revisit, on the other hand, you lose. They are eventually forgotten.

This process of losing un-stimulated, unnecessary memories is called *dendritic pruning*. Dendrites have a fourteen-day half-life. That means that fifty percent dissolve in fourteen days. After twenty-eight days, you'll have lost seventy-five percent of your thoughts. If you take that thought captive, eventually you'll change your thoughts...*unless you stimulate them to keep them alive. See website for dendritic pruning at* www.thekingsprotocol.com

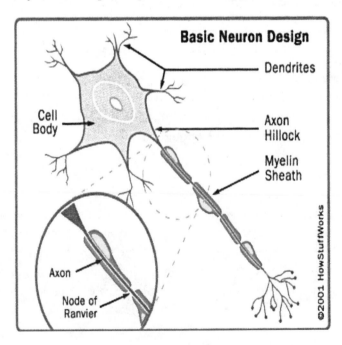

Basic Neuron Design

Dendrites

Cell Body

Axon Hillock

Myelin Sheath

Axon

Node of Ranvier

©2001 HowStuffWorks

So what's the problem with those old thoughts that you don't want? Why weren't they dendritically pruned? The answer is, of course, that they were once important to you. A warning about danger might have been painful, but your brain assumed that this memory was necessary for your survival. You weren't allowed to prune off that one.

Unfortunately, those old and unhelpful dendritic connections have become comfortable in your head. They want to stay alive. If you deprive an old thought by refusing to dwell on it or stimulate it, it will try to stay alive. It will try to fire on its own to keep its place in your brain. *And we can predict exactly when that will happen.* Fourteen days from now, the old thoughts will fight for their right to life.

Is it possible to re-wire your brain so that your old thoughts are reigned in and neutralized? *Yes.* It takes effort, but I have done it, and so have millions of other people. If you want to rewire your brain permanently, you repeat the exercise, again and again, as often as you need to. Your brain can only take two pathways: the fear and bitterness pathway or the faith pathway. The enemy's Kingdom is totally under the fear pathway and God's Kingdom is under the faith pathway. Everything in the enemy's Kingdom—bitterness, resentment, retaliation, anger, and the rest—fits into the fear pathway. God's Kingdom fits into the faith pathway.

Suppose you have visualized your "sinner," the one who hurt you, wearing the *sin* cloak, and you've separated him from the cloak. You've said to him/her, "I forgive you." That new thought, "Forgive him or her," is battling the old thought, "Hate him or her." In two weeks, the old thought, "Hate him or her," will be fighting for its life. It may become frenzied and desperately try to "stimulate" itself into life. However, in another two weeks it will be weaker. It will be easier to defeat with the new forgiveness, though.

Eventually the connection will be automatic. Every time the "Hate" neuron is triggered, it will instantly trigger the "Forgive" neuron with it as part of that thought. The brain will be rewired. The old thought will be taken captive. This is Romans 12:2: "And be not conformed to this world: but be ye transformed by the renewing of your mind, that ye may prove what is that good, and acceptable, and perfect, will of God."

That word "transformed" means metamorphosis, like a caterpillar turning into a butterfly. Does Romans 12:2 finally make sense?

Time-Stamping the Trauma

The only remaining question is, "How do you create the 'new connection'?" Here is a great way to do it: speak the new thought aloud. The thalamus is looking for something in the environment that resembles your old trauma. If it finds something, it presses the PAIN button stored in your amygdala. The thalamus is sensitive to information from the five senses, and it recognizes *your voice*. It takes your words as more authoritative than anyone else's, for the thalamus is the part of your brain that only obeys your voice.

Simply hearing the word isn't going to make a new connection. However, when the thalamus hears your voice saying "That's correct," it registers that the new ideas are indeed correct. So one way to help the capture process is to say, "I forgive you" aloud.

I had my finger cut off when I was twelve years old; it was sewn back on and if you saw my hand you would never know of this trauma. For years afterwards, whenever I remembered this trauma, I relived the exact experience. Whenever I thought about it, I'd actually feel the identical neurological processes repeating themselves. I used to talk about this accident as if it was still happening—because, from my perspective, it was. Then I learned to put a time stamp on that trauma. Whenever the old memory resurfaced, I would speak aloud. I'd say, "I'm no longer twelve years old. I'm forty-eight years old. That's just a memory."

This exercise may sound simple, but it changes the way the brain processes the information it takes it from a trauma memory and stores it as an auditory memory. The thalamus hears your voice and absorbs the message: "This is not the same trauma after all. False match!" The memory is still there, but it is now being stored in a different filing cabinet.

Whenever the thalamus "reads" this file in the future, it does not process the memory as a live trauma that presents a current danger, but as neutral information that has been passed on verbally.

Eventually, the pathway to the *pain* trigger is broken. The memory "feels" like something that happened to someone else. If you have a trauma that you are constantly re-living and feeling, you can put a time stamp on it. Here are some new thoughts that you can speak out loud so that your thalamus knows to match the old connections to new triggers. See the website for the Green Card: www.thekingsprotocol.com. The green card link provides details for dealing with trauma.

The Fiscal Connection

Doubling the income?

When I began teaching seminars on forgiveness all over the USA, (give this to them in the bio) I wasn't even thinking about medical healing, for I had no idea there were so many levels that forgiveness could touch. I was a successful businessman, and I was approaching the problem from the financial perspective. It was clear to me that if people would forgive, their income would increase. It was unmistakable to me that in the parable of the "Unforgiving Servant," Jesus was talking about money, especially at the beginning of the parable.

I used to consult to businesses. I could walk into any business anywhere in the USA, and within a short period of time, I could see why the business wasn't performing at top efficiency. Yet the people running the business could *not* see the problem. These are people that started the business, founded the business, spent their life savings to invest in the business, and run the business every day. They eat, sleep, and drink the business. This is called a "blind spot," and it takes someone from the outside to help them see it. Is it possible that you have a block, that you have that one thing in your life that you are within reach of, and for some reason it escapes you? See the website for a friend to help with a "blind spot." www.thekingsprotocol.com

Everywhere I went, there were financial problems. And since I looked and talked like a successful businessman, I was stopped and told the stories about debt overload, businesses that failed, people facing foreclosure, and so on.

Jose's Story

A man named Jose came to my seminar with his wife. He was a laborer earning $14 per hour as a roofer. He and his wife listened to the teaching. After doing this for over twenty years, I can see the pain and emotions in people's eyes.

Well, the meeting ended. I took Jose and his wife aside and prayed for them. They were crying and repenting. They forgave an aunt whose sins seemed to be like a malignant spider's web, creeping around and harming every member of the family, including Jose and his wife. When they both forgave this aunt, they could no longer stand up. It was as if God had evicted the alien invaders and he began to dwell with them.

What happened next will be forever etched in the heavenly history books.

While I was praying, I said, "You, Jose, are going to get a job that pays you double what you are making right now." It was one of those times when you want to pull the words back, but they rushed out of my mouth so powerfully and with such authority that they were out and out loud before I could stop them. If it had been a cartoon, I would have grabbed that bubble with words in it and erased them, but it was too late.

That was on Friday night. The following Monday morning, instead of going to work, Jose decided to take a vacation day. While he was home reading his Bible, the phone rang and a voice on the other end said, "Jose, did you fill out a job application for my company?"

Jose said, "Yes, but that was six months ago."

"Oh," the voice said. "I was going through the job applications. Yours was on the bottom and I moved it to the top. Can you come down for an interview today?"

Surprised, Jose made good use of his day off by traveling to the office. The interview went well even before the interviewer asked, "Do you know anything about OHSA regulations in roofing?"

As it happened, Jose was very well informed on this point.

"Good," said the interviewer. "We are holding an OHSA class next door in just a few minutes. Would you like to go into the class with the view of taking the test and applying for the OSHA job?"

Jose walked into the classroom, listened to the seminar, took the test, earned the highest grade that had ever been awarded on that test, and was interviewed for the OHSA job *that day*. The employer did not hesitate to offer him the job and told him that it paid $28 an hour.

Jose was so overwhelmed that he lost all control and spluttered. It was like a burst from his—well, never mind. In the pause, as he was wiping it up, the employer asked him what the matter was, and all Jose could say was, "Nobody has ever offered me $28 per hour before."

The employer, not knowing how low Jose's old salary had been, completely misunderstood! "Well, perhaps we can start you on $30 an hour," he said, "and we'll give you a raise in four weeks."

They shook on the deal. As Jose was walking out, his wife called him to ask how it had gone. He could hardly contain his excitement over the good news.

"And they've doubled my paycheck," he finished, "just as Mr. Quental prayed!"

"Jose," she responded, "no one is going to pay you $28 per hour!"

"That's only half the story," he told her. "They went to $30 per hour, and they're going to give me a raise and full benefits!"

I met Jose again a year later. His life had completely changed, and he was still amazed by his good fortune. How do you explain that as soon as Jose forgave his aunt, he coincidentally received a response to his old job application? Unlike some of the other testimonies here, you can trace a direct link between Jose's new attitude and the telephone call. What happened was that when Jose forgave, he finally gave God room to work.

The story of Jose is one of my favorites, but the truth is, I have countless testimonies like this in my files. I could write whole books only about people who have been financially blessed after forgiving, and whole books more about people whose diseases were healed after forgiving.

My point is that similar blessings await you if you forgive.

The Voice of the King

Let us, you and I, get to hearing from the King.

As I told you at the beginning of this book, I began each seminar or conference or church address with these words.

> I'm not a pastor; I'm a businessman. I was trained by the some of the best in the world at business. I experienced a real-life trauma and I am going to share with you what I have learned. The trauma was incredibly painful, the toughest thing a man can go through. This seminar will not be theory; it is practical and powerful. It is time-tested and certain. It works everywhere on the planet. I had so-called incurable illnesses, and they are now gone. How many of you here would like to hear the voice of God in the next five minutes?

This worked for ninety-five percent of the people everywhere I went. They *all* wanted to hear God speaking. In five minutes, they clearly heard the voice of God and acted on it. I had their attention, and God had their hearts.

You see, the King's heart is to hear his people's requests, as in our parable. A man that owed $20 billion came to the King and asked, "Have patience with me and I will pay you all." The King was more than ready to hear and listen and respond. Your enemy will never, ever, ever, ever tell you to forgive someone.

That is your Enemy's Protocol. The King's protocol demands it, and it works every time. You must choose which protocol you will follow: The enemy's, and you'll be turned over to the tormentors, or the King's, and you'll receive the King's blessing and *peace*! Which will it be?

Here is my invitation to you: put everything down; your life is going to change right now. After you read this, close your eyes and ask God the Father to show you whom you need to forgive right now. Do it right now! Close your eyes right now and say out loud, "Father, God, please show me whom I need to forgive." Wait and don't do anything until he shows you.

At the end of the book, we have made available to you a tool to help close the doors that may have opened you to bitterness in your life and your previous generations.

Rarely do we see someone not hear from the King when they ask him to show them whom to forgive. When he or she is so bitter or so full of pride that they won't forgive. If that is the case, go to the end of the book and follow the instructions on the blue card. In addition, if you have been shown whom to forgive, now is the time to close the doors legally to your enemies—bitterness and unforgiveness. Either way, I'm proud of you, and I know your life will be different!

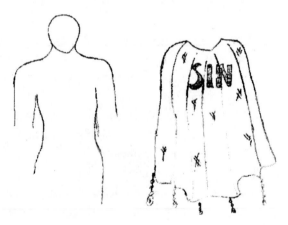

Once the King shows you whom to forgive
Forgive like this…

❑   I forgive you, Dad. I see the sin next to you. It's not you.

- ❑ I forgive you, Mom. I release you from any and all expectations, either real or imagined.
- ❑ I forgive you, ———.
- ❑ I forgive myself. I see the sin next to me. It's not me.
- ❑ I forgive you, God.
- ❑ Romans 7: It's not me, but sin that was living in me.

I want you to take the time to write down each name, and we have a workbook that will help you. Go to the website and download this tool: www.thekingsprotocol.com

Another very important step is a process you will go through 14 days from now. It is called the fourteen-day half-life of the dendrites. I alluded to it earlier. It is critical for you to go through that process in fourteen days. Go to the website and register for a reminder and the tools for the fourteen-day cycle. www.thekingsprotocol.com

Very few ministries understand and use the fourteen-day cycle, and a lot of people lose ground that they have gained by not following through at the fourteen-day cycle. Don't lose ground; go to the book website: www.thekingsprotocol.com

The Blue Card

Order of Ministry

Begin with prayer.
Break the power of each Strongman - e.g., Bitterness.
Deal with each of the underlings.
Then go back and cast out the Strongman - e.g., Bitterness.
If necessary, speak a creative miracle into being.

Strongmen	Underlings
Bitterness	Unforgiveness
Accusing Spirit	Resentment
Trauma	Retaliation
Envy/Jealousy	Anger/Wrath
Rejection	Hate
Unloving Spirit	Violence
Fear	Murder
Occultism	

Remember:
It is all based on
Relationship
and
Recognizing.

● **Father God** - I take *responsibility* for the spirit of XX in my generation and all previous generations on both my mother's and my father's side all the way back to Adam.
● I *repent* of and *renounce* the spirit of XX.
● I ask *forgiveness* for allowing XX in my life and cooperating with it. I receive your forgiveness and I forgive myself.
● I ask now that the curse be cancelled.

● In the name of Jesus of Nazareth, by the power of the Holy Spirit -
● I take *authority* over you, spirit of XX.   (Recorder Spirit also)
● I *break your power,* spirit of XX and *cancel* your assignment.
● I *cast you out* spirit of XX and *consign* you to the dry places.

● Father God, *heal* the place where the spirit of XX has been and *fill* that place with Yourself...   (Programming)

Appendix

Atrial Natriuretic Peptide

"Atrial natriuretic peptide (ANP), atrial natriuretic factor (ANF), atrial natriuretic hormone (ANH), Cardionatrine, Cardiodilatine (CDD) or atriopeptin, is a powerful vasodilator, and a protein (polypeptide) hormone secreted by heart muscle cells. It is involved in the homeostatic control of body water, sodium, potassium and fat (adipose tissue). It is released by muscle cells in the upper chambers (atria) of the heart (atrial myocytes) in response to high blood pressure. ANP acts to reduce the water, sodium and adipose loads on the circulatory system, thereby reducing blood pressure" (Wikipedia).

Beriberi

"Beriberi refers to a cluster of symptoms caused primarily by a nutritional deficit in Vitamin B1 (thiamine). Beriberi has conventionally been divided into three separate entities, relating to the body system involved (nervous or cardiovascular) or age of patient (infantile). Beriberi is one of several thiamine-deficiency related conditions, which may occur concurrently, including Wernicke's encephalopathy, Korsakoff's syndrome, and Wernicke-Korsakoff syndrome.

Historically, Beriberi has been endemic in regions dependent on what is variously referred to as polished, white, or de-husked rice. This type of rice has its husk removed in order to extend its lifespan, but also has the unintended side-effect of removing the primary source of thiamine" (Wikipedia).

Bibliography

Leaf, Caroline. Dr. Caroline Leaf, "Dr. Leaf, Switch on Your Brain." Last modified 2013. Accessed October 23, 2013. *http://www.drleaf.com/index.php.*

Mayo Clinic Staff. The Mayo Clinic, "Forgiveness: Letting go of grudges and bitterness." Accessed October 23, 2013. *http://www.mayoclinic.com/health/forgiveness/MH00131*

Wikipedia Foundation, Inc., "Atrial natriuretic peptide." Last modified October 16, 2013. Accessed October 23, 2013. *http://en.wikipedia.org/wiki/Atrial_natriuretic_peptide*

Wikipedia Foundation, Inc., "Beriberi." Last modified October 02, 2013. Accessed October 23, 2013. *http://en.wikipedia. org/wiki/Beriberi.*